CATS

WHO CHANGED THE WORLD

CATS

WHO CHANGED
THE WORLD

DAN
JONES

50 cats who altered history,
inspired literature ... or ruined everything

INTRODUCTION

Cats are weird. In the thousands of years they have lived alongside us, weaving in between our shins and offering themselves up for treats and a clean litter tray, the cat has inveigled its way into the lives and loves of humankind. The bond between feline and human is undeniable, and they are adored and revered by almost every culture. But still . . . they are weird.

The cat will happily ignore its owner to jump into the lap of those that can't quite bear them, triggering allergies or delivering the mangled corpse of a mouse. Thirsty? They will dip a paw in your last glass of water. Sleepy? They'll knock over a plant pot at 3am and then mewl outside your bedroom door as the sun rises. It's as if they can see inside your mind. No wonder they have long been suspected of having supernatural, satanic powers. Their indifference knows no bounds: while a dog might drag you from a burning building, a cat might lick its butthole while you go up in flames.

All this is not to do the cat a disservice, and it is easy to pit canines and felines against each other. But, in acknowledging cat-weirdness, we can underline how truly magical it is when they do indeed fall in love with you. What's more, their incredible acts of bravery, inspiration and survival can be truly awe-inspiring in their unlikeliness.

Through 50 stories, this book is a celebration of the not-so-humble cat in all its sharp-clawed glory. Meet the cats who inspired great artists and musicians, from Andy Warhol and Salvador Dalí to Carole King and Joni Mitchell, and those felines who inspired literary greats, like Edgar Allan Poe's darling Catterina, C. S. Lewis's *Cheshire Cat* and Hemingway's cat colonies. Others have predicted the future to avoid bomb strikes in the Blitz or sensed when a human is about to pass away. There is Snowball, who helped solve a murder in a remote island community; Tama, the cat that oversees a railway service that reinvigorated a town; and Mačak, who inspired

Nikola Tesla to follow his passion for electricity and make his most important discoveries.

Meet feline war heroes, film stars, record-breaking mouse-killers and cat-fighters of homophobia. And discover other cats of note who have not been quite as heroic or helpful – there are cat-clones, cats with the power of human mind-control, wise-cracking witches' familiars and alien-fighting reluctant movie stars. One slaughtered an entire species, and others simply won awards as being the oldest, hairiest or grumpiest cats in the world. And at least one is famous for getting (accidentally) high with Nicolas Cage.

Cats have always walked the line between self-sufficiency and neediness, padding delicately into the lives of their chosen human, who becomes both their guardian and servant. Life with a cat is not easy, and even the most-loved cat owner is often covered in scratches, and yet we adore them (there are few things more heart-breaking than whispering "pspsps" to a cat and being ignored). These 50 stories remind us of the true nature of this independent, mysterious animal that looms as large in ancient myth and legend as it does in our own living rooms. If they have any message for us at all, it is surely to "stay weird".

FÉLICETTE

THE FIRST FELINE IN SPACE

MOGGY

In the 1960s France was keen to set its first paw in space. The nation's Centre d'Enseignement et de Recherches de Médecine Aéronautique (CERMA) had already sent three live rats into the stratosphere, but the more complicated task of feline re-entry was its goal. CERMA scientists herded 14 cats through a gruelling training programme, waiting to see which feline astronaut would shine out. They found their hero in "tuxedo cat" Félicette, a small black and white former stray. So, in 1963 they set about sending her to the stars.

Félicette had spent her early years delicately sniffing and scavenging the aromatic alleyways of Paris before finding herself as France's best hope of winning the space race. In 1957 the Russians had already sent a dog, Laika, into orbit (although the tragic end – poor Laika was never meant to return alive – somewhat dampened public support for space exploration), followed by Ham, a chimpanzee, in 1961. Now it was French Félicette's turn. From the launch site in Hammaguir, Algeria, Félicette (then known by the moniker C341) was strapped inside a Véronique rocket and blasted off for a suborbital trip of five minutes of weightlessness, returning to Earth moments later.

Much like Laika, little Félicette's vitals were measured via medical implants and, although she made it home unscathed, she met an abrupt end at the hands of CERMA for vivisection a few months after arriving home. From a contemporary viewpoint, space exploration and animal rights have long had something of a

toxic relationship. Are animals truly expendable in the pursuit of scientific endeavour? Should we test our own human safety with the living bodies of our animal friends? For all their heroic places in history, intergalactic animals have suffered greatly for our own gains; creatures like Félicette and her training mates were a casualty in our feverish need to go where no cat has gone before.

Although celebrated at the time, Félicette's sacrifice soon slipped from the public consciousness . . . until the rediscovery of her story in recent times. A publicly funded bronze statue by sculptor Gill Parker was unveiled in 2019 at the International Space University near Strasbourg, 250 miles from Paris, where France's best-travelled cat spent her prowling years. The bronze statue depicts little Félicette perched upon the Earth, sniffing up at the stars.

CHOUPETTE

THE LEGENDARY BIRMAN CAT OF KARL LAGERFELD

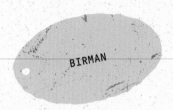

BIRMAN

The greatest artists, composers and designers are enslaved to their muses, and the relationship between Karl Lagerfeld (1933–2019) and Choupette was indeed one of utter devotion, indulgence and inspiration. When the legendary fashion designer and man-at-the-helm of Chanel first saw Choupette's pale sapphire eyes, smoky grey fur and delicate, quizzical face, his world was transformed. With his infamous icy demeanour, which was a longstanding part of his personal brand, many of the designer's friends and fans were shocked at how a simple Birman cat melted Lagerfeld's heart.

Born on 15 August 2011, Choupette originally belonged to Baptiste Giabiconi, a thrillingly handsome French model who had been gifted the pompom-like Birman kitten as a birthday treat, and it was Baptiste who named her Choupette. Months later, Lagerfeld was tasked with looking after the cat while Baptiste took a brief Christmas trip, but when he returned to collect Choupette, all was not well in *chez* Lagerfeld. Baptiste initially struggled to understand his friend's grumpiness, but within a week it had dawned on him what he had to do. He knocked on Karl's front door and handed over Choupette, who had clearly become indispensable to the fabled designer. Lagerfeld was delighted: he had been reunited with this unexpected muse. But it was Stephen Gan of *V* magazine who inadvertently made Choupette the star she was always going to be. Posting an image of the kitten taken at Lagerfeld's apartment, the story of a titan of design and his newfound love of a cute kitten went viral. Soon Choupette became her own brand – a sort of kitty influencer, with

lucrative makeup lines, face-print handbags and Chanel's "Choupette blue" accessories. Lagerfeld treated her to shoots and fashion spreads in glossy magazines, flights on a private jet, dinners on Goyard plates and two devoted cat-nannies.

After his death at the age of 85, rumours abounded about on whom he had bestowed his considerable fortune. One word was on the lips of fashion reporters and industry insiders, "Choupette!", but Lagerfeld's people were tight-lipped. Fans of the petite Birman were distraught, visiting Chanel stores to pay their respects to Lagerfeld, but also to ask the question: what would happen to the grieving cat herself?

Luckily Choupette had her own agent, and her life continued just as Lagerfeld himself would have wanted. A book of Lagerfeld's portraits of Choupette, published by Steidl and bound in a luxury blue fabric to match her eyes, was released in 2019 and, if reports are true, the cat now lives comfortably and quietly with one of her original cat-nannies, no doubt endlessly pining for her dad.

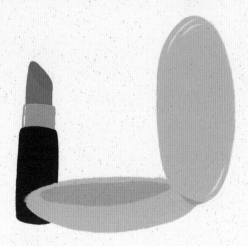

COLETTE'S CATS

LA CHATTE AND A LITERARY LEGEND

French icon Colette (1873–1954), aka Sidonie-Gabrielle Colette (but known by a mononym like other creative greats such as Shakespeare, Chaucer and Cher) was the most important novelist, journalist, performer, *bon vivant* and cat-lover of *fin-de-siècle* Paris. Like most successful, outspoken women, everyone has an opinion about her, from her sizzling scandals and lesbian relationships (Colette had both male and female lovers) to becoming a "frizzle-headed cat woman of the 20th century" (written by lit critic Terry Castle, and a description we can all respect).

Cats were sacred to Colette, especially in her later years. Each enjoyed the status of being main characters not only in her day-to-day life, but also in her writing. In short-story collection *Dialogues de bêtes*, Colette lays bare her animal obsessions through her two leads: a cat, Kiki-la-Doucette, and a dog, Toby-Chien. Her most famous novel, *Gigi*, was turned into a musical and Academy-award winning film of 1958, but it's her murderous love-triangle novella

La Chatte that might be her most curious work – and it certainly underlines her feline love. The love triangle in *La Chatte* is between Alain, a woman and a cat, Saha, who nearly (but thankfully doesn't) meets a grisly end. Alain is in love with Saha – a gorgeous Chartreux, inspired by Colette's own childhood cat known as La Chatte – and ignores his beautiful new wife in the process. The "pearl-coloured demon", as Alain calls his cat, proceeds to "trample delicately on her friend's chest" in the dark. "Each time she pressed down her feet, one single claw pierced the silk of the pyjamas, catching the skin just enough for Alain to feel an uneasy pleasure." Each slinky step and each carefully placed paw becomes a signifier for female sexuality and desire. Never come between a cat lover and their cat!

Colette's freewheeling approach to life, love and husbands, and her frothy, glamorous works, belied her efforts to hide and help Jewish people, including her husband, in occupied France. Truly a cat-loving literary legend.

CHARTREUX

SOCKS

MOGGY

Alongside the top secret, world-altering political decisions, thrilling scandals and festive decoration controversies, the grand old house at 1600 Pennsylvania Avenue in Washington, DC, has also been home to a menagerie of lauded cats and dogs. As the president's residence and epicentre of the free world since 1800, the White House has always welcomed the beloved pets of its presidential staff and families. One such political heavyweight is Socks, the Clinton dynasty's black-and-white-pawed cat.

Socks jumped into the Clinton's lives, literally. Legend has it that, on leaving Little Rock, Arkansas, the then stray jumped into the arms of First Daughter Chelsea Clinton, declaring her his human. On moving to the White House, Socks was, by all reports, a sociable fellow, sharing 1600 Pennsylvania Ave with the Clinton's dog, Buddy, and a stray cat nicknamed Slippers.

"First Cats" are vanishingly rare in the White House; only a dozen or so have padded the carpeted halls of power compared to around 100 dogs (and the Kennedy's earnest little pony, Macaroni). Socks soon became a celebrity of sorts, with a children's book, graphic novel, video game, set of Central West African postage stamps and a fashion brand. Socks was basically the first cat influencer.

He didn't let fame go to his head, though. He spent his days swishing about the usher's office, claiming the window heater as his own, waiting for President Bill Clinton to visit on his way to the Oval Office. Socks was lucky: although the Roosevelt's cat haunted the kitchen, and Herbert Hoover's prissy Persian had free rein to roam and butt-lick in inappropriate places, most presidential cats are usually confined to the family residence.

Soon Socks found a new object of affection in Betty Currie, the president's personal secretary. It was just as well as, after five years of bliss, Socks was knocked off the top spot by the arrival of his new arch nemesis, a dog named Buddy. *The Washington Post* reported that, when Bill Clinton introduced Socks to his new chocolate lab puppy on the White House lawn, it was "hate at first sight, and relations never improved". The pair co-existed painfully until Bill Clinton left office in 2001 and Socks moved to Maryland with his beloved Betty. He ended his days with her, never having to see his enemy again. Just before his exit, Clinton told CNN, "You know, I did better with the Arabs, the Palestinians and the Israelis than I've done with Socks and Buddy."

SOCKS

UNSINKABLE SAM

THE UNSINKABLE CAT WITH A KNACK FOR SINKING SHIPS

Proof that cats do have nine lives – or at least three – is Unsinkable Sam, the seafaring cat. Sam, originally called Oscar, first came to notoriety on the sinking of the warship *Bismarck* in the Second World War on 18 May 1941. The tiny black-and-white "tuxedo" cat was found in the wreckage of the infamous Kriegsmarine vessel, bobbing along on a board, and soon Sam was scooped up by British forces. Impressed with his tenacity, sailors installed him on *HMS Cossack* for good luck.

Sam soon settled into life on board the British vessel and carried out escort duties in the Mediterranean and beyond for many months, but if the crew thought Sam's inherent luck might rub off on them, they were sadly mistaken. On 24 October 1941, the *Cossack* took a direct torpedo hit and, severely damaged, sank a few days later. Sam was evacuated with many of the surviving crew and was taken ashore in Gibraltar. It was there the small, affable feline earned the title "Unsinkable Sam", and he was soon

sent on another Allied mission, this time on board *HMS Ark Royal*, an aircraft carrier that had been part of the fierce gun battle that saw the demise of the *Bismarck*.

Unsinkable Sam was thought of as a good-luck mascot, imbuing any vessel he trod his paws on with near-magical properties. No one, it seemed, questioned what might have been the dark reality of Sam's life, that of sinking any ship he plodded on. Just weeks after his escape from the *Cossack*, Sam found himself part of the evacuation of the *Ark Royal*, which had suffered a torpedo hit on its way back to port. Suspiciously, Sam survived once more, the legend of his unsinkable status set forever.

Sam lived out the rest of his days in comfort with his seaman friends at the Home for Sailors in Belfast. Who knows what deathly acts he committed there before he passed away in 1955? Such stories are lost to the mists of time. In fact, some historians question whether Sam existed at all, but isn't that *just* what a catastrophe-inducing cat would want you to think?

No 6

FREDDIE MERCURY'S FELINES

DON'T STOP THEM NOW,
THEY'RE HAVING SUCH A GOOD TIME

A look through pictures of Freddie Mercury, the delightfully camp original frontman of legendary pop-rock outfit Queen, will reveal dozens of sequined one-pieces (cut scandalously low), bulging tight-tights and wet-look leather . . . and more than a few cats. The toothy showman became feline-obsessed after his 1970s girlfriend Mary Austin brought home Tom and Jerry, a pair of delightful cats. It was a kind of magic, and Mercury was suddenly in a crazy little thing called love. On tour with Queen, Mercury would call Austin and, like all true cat lovers, she would hold the receiver up to each cat's ear so Mercury could chat with them.

Over the years, Mercury added more to the family with Tiffany, Dorothy, Delilah, Goliath, Lily, Miko, Oscar and Romeo joining pack-leaders Tom and Jerry. They were delightfully cosseted, each with his or her own Christmas stocking packed with treats and toys. Queen fans (known as the most loyal of all pop and rock fans of that era) also fell in love with Mercury's brood and would send gifts for their favourites.

Having such a large cat entourage was not all (bohemian) rhapsody, though, with 10 fractious feline personalities to be catered for. One cat proved more demanding to Mercury than the others, but the relationship was not without its rewards. On *Innuendo*, the band's final album in Freddie's lifetime, is an ode to the prissiest of Mercury's cats, Delilah. The eponymously titled track details Mercury and Delilah's sub-dom relationship: "You make me so very happy / When you cuddle up and go to sleep beside me / And then you make me slightly mad / When you pee all over my Chippendale suite." A typical human-cat relationship if you will; a furry story of love and destruction. Anyway, don't stop me now, because the show must go on. (Sorry, I'll stop.)

24   FREDDIE MERCURY'S FELINES

ORANGEY

THE *BREAKFAST AT TIFFANY'S* FELINE ACTOR

TABBY

Isn't it always delicious to hear that a celebrity is secretly horrible? Meet award-winning acting feline Orangey, aka "the world's meanest cat" and marmalade tabby tom star of *Breakfast at Tiffany's*. As a working actor in the 1950s and '60s, Orangey sniffed out a series of high-profile roles, including in *Batman*, *Mission Impossible* and his star turn lounging in the arms of Audrey Hepburn as "Cat" in *Breakfast at Tiffany's*.

Much has been made of Orangey's short-tempered personality. According to his award-winning cinematic animal handler, Frank Inn, he might scratch and hiss at his fellow actors and then, tail high, enact a daring escape, halting on-set production for hours at a time. Perhaps this attitude is what won him the role of Cat in *Tiffany's*; Orangey certainly had the countenance of a no-nonsense New Yorker.

It was an unnamed studio exec who declared Orangey the "world's meanest", but working on set can be a tense, laborious business . . . perhaps Orangey was just expressing his frustration? And reports of dogs being installed at the studio gates to thwart Orangey's escapes seem excessive. Nevertheless, his attitude didn't stop him scoring the best roles and awards. Orangey won two Patsys in his lifetime (Picture Animal Top Star of the Year, the animal equivalent of the Oscars, apparently), acted alongside Eartha Kitt's Catwoman in *Batman* and was uncharacteristically floppy in tough Emile Meyer's arms in the Western *Stranger on Horseback* (1955), leading some to suspect Orangey was occasionally replaced with a series of feline lookalikes. Inn's own recollection seems to confirm this. In *Rhubarb* (1951), Orangey's first feature

film, in which a cat inherits a baseball team, Inn revealed he used more than 30 lookalike cats, each with one or two tricks at their disposal, but only Orangey was credited.

Inn, a lifelong animal lover, managed a huge coterie of cats and other performing animals, caring for the ones too elderly to perform in a sort of unofficial sanctuary. It wasn't just a business for Inn as much as a genuine love of working pets like Orangey; the handler even had plans to be buried with his favourite ex-cats' ashes. In the end, Orangey seems to have enjoyed a sort of primary cat status, with other marmalade felines considered stand-ins, like so many other Hollywood starlets-in-waiting.

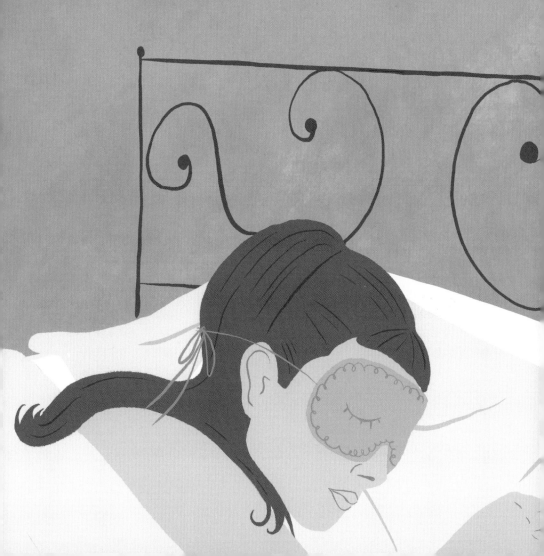

MAČAK

NIKOLA TESLA'S ELECTRIC CAT

Nikola Tesla (1856–1943) was the maverick engineer and inventor who dazzled the world with his electrifying know-how. The Serbian-American was a showman, enthralling celebrity audiences with his incredible live experiments, all underpinned by his odd obsessions (he loved pigeons and the number 3, detested earrings) and endless competitiveness. He was always just one step away from his biggest, best idea.

As a contemporary of Thomas Edison and Guglielmo Marconi, Tesla raced to prove and patent his ideas and electrical inventions, from his famous "Tesla coil" to neon lights, radio and the first alternating current motor. But what had originally inspired this maverick of science? A simple black cat named Mačak.

In 1939 Tesla wrote a letter to a 12-year-old science geek, Pola Fottich, in which he divulged just what had ignited his lifelong fascination with electricity: his childhood pet. "In the dusk of the evening as I stroked Mačak's back," Tesla wrote to Pola, "I saw a miracle which made me speechless with amazement. Mačak's back was a sheet of light, and my hand produced a shower of crackling sparks loud enough to be heard all over the house ... I cannot exaggerate the effect of this marvellous night on my childish imagination. Day after day I have asked myself, what is electricity?"

Tesla's letter is nothing short of charming, offering Pola a fantastical yarn that no doubt delighted the young STEM student and would encourage any child's interest in all things electric. Would Tesla have set out on the same ingenious, world-changing course had Mačak the electric cat not sparked such an interest? We may never know, but it's a shockingly good story.

MOGGY

TAMA

Little Tama was born in Kinokawa, a sleepy town south of Osaka that had fought to keep its tiny local train station open – and which lived with the constant worry it would one day close. All this might have seemed uninteresting to the average cat, but not Tama. In the late 1990s the calico-coloured cat lived with a pack of strays that would pad about Kishi station, but she soon levelled up to be unofficially adopted by Toshiko Koyama, the part-time station master, and became a firm favourite of the Kinokawa locals. Then in 2007 something extraordinary happened: Tama accepted the position of station master, under Koyama's watchful eye.

There is something delightful when an otherwise staid, practical public organisation recognises the special role of a cat, and Tama certainly excelled at her role of greeting passengers. In fact, she became something of a celebrity: news of her appointment spread, including the details of her wage (one year's worth of cat food and a golden pet tag, if you're interested) – and the tiny station master's hat she was issued with is, let's face it, an almost unbearably cute idea. Most importantly, Tama's fame had incredible consequences. She helped

transform the once-ailing station, with passenger numbers jumping up dramatically by more than 10% in one year, and it is thought Tama created millions of yen for the local community. In fact, the figures were so astounding that Tama became a test case in the study of "*Nekonomics*" (aka the cat economy). She had saved Kishi station and the community of Kinokawa.

Tama was promoted again and again, each with its own small ceremony and celebratory treat (a morsel of crab), and her fame grew and grew. Soon a Tama-themed train appeared on the tracks (with a cat's face), and in 2010 Kishi station was redesigned by architect Eiji Mitooka, who added two Tama-like cat's-eye windows winking out of its sloping roof. Soon more cats joined the now famous Kishigawa railway line as mascots.

In her later years, Tama was allowed time away from her adoring fans and, when she passed away in 2015, thousands of Tama-fans paid their respects at a rare Shinto-style funeral. She is now regarded as an Honorary Eternal Stationmaster, a fitting acknowledgement to the cat who saved a community.

STUBBS

THE ALMOST-MAYOR OF TALKEETNA

TABBY

To Alaska and the small town of Talkeetna, some 115 miles north of Anchorage. Meet Stubbs (1997–2017), a delicious-looking marmalade tabby who many claim was the one-time mayor.

Stubbs had a lowly beginning: one of a litter of kittens discovered in a cardboard box in 1997 near Nagley's, a popular general store. He was adopted, named Stubbs (because of his stubby tail) and became quite the cat about town. He was soon known as "the Fonzie of cats in Talkeetna" in reference to the super-smooth character of retro American sitcom *Happy Days*.

A popular presence, he seemed to have the run of Talkeetna, from hitching a ride on a garbage truck to entering restaurant kitchens (he once fell into a deep fat fryer, thankfully switched off at the time), but it was in politics that Stubbs made his name. *TIME* magazine reported on him in 2012, pondering if the small Alaskan town had fixed politics by electing a cat mayor, ensuring him an impressive 15-year reign. The story went as thus: dissatisfied with their local representatives, Talkeetna residents undertook a write-in campaign for Stubbs to preside over the town, and duly elected their favourite cat as leader.

Having a cat-mayor put Talkeetna on the map, garnered numerous positive (if bemused) press pieces, and tourists soon started dropping by in the hope to meet him. But not everyone was enamoured with the delightful tale of a cat-mayor. In 2016 the *Anchorage Daily News* – with its claws out – published a hissing riposte to the cat-frenzy of Talkeetna. "Enough with the cat crap", it wrote, pointing out that the town had never held a write-in campaign, the mayoral candidates were not *so* unliked that townsfolk thought a cat could do a better job, and that Stubbs was not even an honorary mayor: he was simply an enigmatic local stray, albeit a much-loved one. But who cares about facts when the story is as cute and cat-centric as this?

CASPER

THE COMMUTING CAT

To Plymouth, the salty Devonshire port city at the far reaches of southern England, famous for its Brutalist shopping district, one-time mayor Sir Francis Drake and local love of steak pasties. Enter Casper, the long-haired black, white and tan cat, adopted from a pet rescue centre in 2002 into the arms of local cat lady Susan Finden. Almost immediately, Casper began his adventures.

At first, Finden noticed Casper would leave home and return an hour later, but where he went was a mystery. Months later, he followed Finden to the local bus stop, where a bus driver told her that all the local drivers had regularly been giving Casper a ride. The adventurous cat would wait patiently at his local bus stop, hop on the No. 3, and then sit quietly at the front of the bus for the 11-mile round trip before being dropped off safely at home. The story hit the local press, soon went viral and Casper became something of a feline sensation.

After Casper's untimely death in 2010 after a hit-and-run accident, the story of the commuting cat caught the eye of commissioning editors at publishers Simon & Schuster, who quickly purchased the rights to the story and, in August that year, Finden's book *Casper the Commuting Cat* (written with author Linda Watson-Brown) hit the shelves. Translated into six other languages, Casper's story became an international bestseller, raising awareness of pet adoption and the peculiarly self-focused nature of cats.

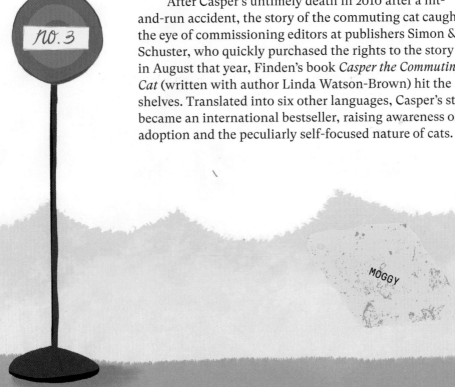

MOGGY

LITTLE NICKY

THE CLONED CAT

MAINE COON

True love never dies – not when a cat is involved. And one such adored cat, Nicky, a stately Maine Coon, inspired an incredible feat of science. Nicky lived for 17 long years of love and luxury in Texas until he passed away in 2003. It was then that his owner, known only as Julie, set about bringing him back to life.

The Maine Coon cat has a fascinating folk history, but few can agree on its true beginnings, and the field of cat genealogy is gossipy and rivalrous. The most audacious origin story is that a boat commissioned for Marie Antoinette's doomed attempted-escape voyage – laden with her favourite things, including several rare cats – reached the shores of New England without her. On being set free, the cats soon set about on an amorous rampage with local cats, and the Maine Coon was born. Descendants of lusty French royalty or not, one thing's for sure: the Maine is big. Really big. The large-framed cats are thought to be the biggest domestic cat, a long- or medium-haired breed known for its exceptional hunting skills and sociable, affectionate nature. Flash forward to modern times, and Nicky was no exception, and Julie, his human, loved him dearly.

Enter Genetic Savings & Clone, Inc., a private company that, in conjunction with the Texas A&M University, sought to add another chapter to the Maine Coon's intriguing history. This time, the fantastical cat would be cloned. The company had already had success with cloning a cat in 2001, a little tabby known as CC (aka Carbon Copy) and launched its consumer cloning service in 2004. After

Nicky's death, Julie sent off tissue samples to Genetic Savings' pet bank and soon became their first customer. Julie paid approximately $50,000 for the company to re-animate her beloved. Little Nicky was born in December 2004: the world's first commercially cloned pet and Nicky's official replacement.

"He looks identical," said Julie on *Good Morning America*. "His personality is extremely similar; they are very close." Months later, another clone, Little Gizmo was born. In the press ethical questions abounded. Why go to such great lengths to create a new cat when so many already living are abandoned? And are the rights of the surrogate cat considered in our quest to be reunited with our loved ones? Genetic Savings closed in 2006, with Little Nicky and its other successful clones outliving the company that created them. Love may never die, but it does make us do crazy things.

LITTLE NICKY

SNOWBALL

THE CAT WHO CAUGHT A MURDERER

To the red-sand beaches of King Edward Island, Canada, and the sterling work of Snowball, the white-furred cat who assisted the Royal Canadian Mounted Police in solving a gruesome murder. In 1994 police discovered the abandoned car of a local mother of five who had gone missing days earlier. The car, splattered with her blood, was otherwise empty.

Six months later the police's worst fears were confirmed. A military team stumbled upon her body in a shallow grave just six miles from her house in Summerside; it was murder most horrid. At the scene was a leather jacket, stained with blood, and several tiny strands of white hair. In their investigations the RCMP had noted the woman's ex-partner lived with his parents in nearby Prince County and had a white cat called Snowball – so they soon seized the little feline for evidence.

At first none of the police-affiliated DNA labs would help; they were dumbfounded with the task of identifying a mere cat.

But police inspector Roger Savoie persisted and found his science heroes in the US-based Laboratory of Genomic Diversity, a genetic disease lab at the National Cancer Institute. Officers hoped to prove the hairs belonged to Snowball, placing the suspect at the scene of the crime. By the early/mid 1990s, using DNA evidence in criminal trials was less than a decade old and the lab had to develop a method to test a sample from Snowball using STR (Short Tandem Repeat) genotyping. To rule out other animals, the RCMP also tested 19 local cats and others from around the United States to prove that the feline DNA in question was unique. As the test results arrived, Savoie was confident he had his cat – and his man. "Without the cat, the case falls flat," the defence lawyer, John L. MacDougall, told the jury at trial, but Snowball came good. In fact, the cat was the first non-human DNA evidence used in a criminal trial anywhere in the world. The woman's murderer was convicted of second-degree murder. Justice served.

MOGGY

TIBBLES

THE LIGHTHOUSE KEEPER'S CUTE KILLER

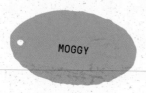

MOGGY

To the tiny, 1.5-square-kilometre island of Takapourewa off the northerly tip of the South Island of New Zealand. Takapourewa is abundant with rare birds, amphibians, insects and reptiles, all protected by New Zealand's world-class biosecurity rules . . . although one species is sadly no longer part of the island family.

In the late 1890s the Lyall's wren was resident on the island, with Takapourewa its final refuge from extinction. The tiny flightless passerine bird was named after assistant lighthouse keeper David Lyall, who first brought the species to the attention of naturalists. In fact, the little wren had once been prevalent in New Zealand prior to the Maori settling there but had been all but snapped up by an invasive species of rat.

Having moved onto the island during the construction of a lighthouse in 1894, cat Tibbles had the run of the island, amusing herself by doing what she did best: chasing, pouncing and mangling all manner of birds before gifting them to the lighthouse keepers. This was how David Lyall was able to identify the thought-to-be-extinct species, but Tibbles, it seems, was too good at her job and it is thought she caught every last one, wiping out the species in one final pounce.

Some dispute Tibbles' species-killing prowess and point out that she was pregnant when she arrived on the island. Soon, it wasn't just Tibbles who snacked on the wrens, but a pack of feral felines descended from her kittens.

Today, Takapourewa is still a stronghold of rare species, and Tibbles' reign is long over. The island is where Hamilton's frog and the Nagao weevil first evolved, and the tuatara – a 60-million-year-old prehistoric lizard-type reptile – can now bask in the sun without the threat of Tibbles ever stalking up behind it.

OSCAR

THE ADORABLE LITTLE HARBINGER OF DEATH

A brief detour to ancient Greece and the priestess Cassandra, who was bestowed with the gift of prophecy but cursed always to be doubted. Aeons later on Rhode Island, NY, lived a cat named Oscar, who seemed to possess a similar gift – only this time, the prophesier was believed.

Dating back to 1874, Steere House Nursing and Rehabilitation Center in Providence is home to those living with late-stage dementia, where they are prescribed skilful nursing, personalised care, love and attention. Part of the home's unique approach was the addition of Oscar (2005–2022), a handsome tortoiseshell-and-white dementia-companion cat who made his home at the pet-friendly facility. Oscar could be found padding about the dementia unit, trying to avoid his companionship duties (he was not a human-loving feline) and instead trying to wrangle treats and catnip. Oscar had been at Steere for around six months when staff noticed something extraordinary: the normally aloof cat would be found curled up with a particularly poorly resident during their final hours.

Dr David Dosa was intrigued. His book *Making Rounds with Oscar: the Extraordinary Gift of an Ordinary Cat* was a *New York Times* bestseller and attempts to unpick the mystery and celebrate Oscar's uncanny gift of predicting the deaths of more than 50 residents over the years (or, as some say, as many as 100). He would scratch on the door of certain residents soon to pass away, asking to be let in, and would jump off the beds of sick residents who went on to recover, proving medics wrong in some cases. Dosa's theory is that Oscar might have been capable, like certain dogs who can detect illness in humans, of detecting ketones, the biochemicals given off by dying cells.

Not only did Oscar's story inspire Dosa's book but also a cat in Stephen King's novel *Doctor Sleep*, and talk of a green-lit Oscar-focused movie has abounded for years. Oscar also gave some solace to the relatives of those who Oscar kept company in their final hours; he was celebrated in numerous newspaper death notices and eulogies.

CATTERINA

THE CREEPY MUSE OF EDGAR ALLAN POE

MOGGY

Haunted radical writer, poet and snarky critic Edgar Allan Poe (1809–1849), author of *The Pit and the Pendulum*, *The Fall of the House of Usher* and *The Raven*, was obsessed with his own tiny feline muse, Catterina (aka Catters). The tortoiseshell cat would perch, draped over his shoulders, as he wrote his romantic masterpieces, overseeing work that, in Poe's later years, was soaked with death and the macabre – so far, so gothic. In fact, much of our contemporary spooky iconography can be traced back to Poe's mournful writings. "Deep into that darkness peering," he wrote, with Catterina on his delicate shoulder, "long I stood there, wondering, fearing, doubting, dreaming dreams no mortal ever dared to dream before."

In Poe's short story *The Black Cat*, he conjures a truly horrific spectacle: the narrator, a lover of cats, somehow descends into abusing them, but they ultimately prove to be his downfall. The short story plays with the power of guilt, reason giving way to madness and the superstitious power of the black cat in folk history – with plenty of spooky goings on too. And Catterina looms large: in Poe's essay *Instinct vs Reason – a Black Cat*, Poe claims: "The writer of this article is the owner of one of the most remarkable black cats in the world – and this is saying much; for it will be remembered that black cats are all of them witches."

Whether Catterina was indeed a witch or just a writers' muse is hard to say, but without her we may have gone without Poe's creepiest stories and poems, works that inspired so many of the writers, filmmakers and artists who followed in his footsteps. What we can say for sure is that there is something truly magical about cats.

TRIPPY LEWIS

THE PSYCHEDELIC CAT OF NICOLAS CAGE

Nicolas Cage, star of *National Treasure: Book of Secrets*, *Con Air* and *Face/Off* (and perhaps the world's finest actor), had an adorable partner in crime: his somewhat errant cat, Lewis. The pair did everything together, even mushrooms . . . or so the legend goes. One day, Cage discovered his cat had pilfered his mushroom stash. "Louis, you can't do that," remonstrated Cage, but it was too late. The cat had eaten them "voraciously", as Cage told Letterman in 2010. "It was like catnip to him. So, I thought what the heck, I'd better do it with him."

Cage and Lewis, it turns out, were perfect mushroom buddies. "I remember lying in my bed for hours," said Cage, "and Lewis was on the desk across from the bed for hours, staring at each other . . . not moving. But he would stare at me, and I had no doubt that he was my brother."

It was Lewis with whom Cage roomed while filming comedy horror *Vampire's Kiss* (1989). The actor was known for rehearsing alone in his hotel room with Lewis by his side. As filming continued, Lewis slowly and methodically destroyed the room as only cats can do. "[The cat] wrecked the whole place," said director Robert Bierman on the film's DVD release. "I remember going up there, and I thought, Jesus, what was Nic doing? Because it was completely wrecked. The cat had pulled everything apart."

Cage also drew inspiration on his relationship with his beloved cat for the character of Rob in *Pig* (2021), a loner who eschews human company in favour of animals and must contend with the disappearance of his porcine friend. Nightmares about losing Lewis helped Cage fuel the role. "I've had those moments where I don't want to be around people," he said on the film's release, "I just want to be with my cat." A sentiment all feline-fans understand, for there is no FOMO with a cat waiting at home. "It's not just . . . a pet," said Cage, "it's your best friend, it's your family. It's pure love, and connection, and companionship."

MOGGY

BASTET

THE SERPENT-SLAYING CAT GODDESS OF ANCIENT EGYPT

GODDESS

Meet Bastet, the goddess of all cats and one of the most-beloved deities of the Egyptian Pantheon. Despite her popularity, she has, like all the best cat-people, a past. Although the etymology of her name is lost to the kitty litter tray of time, in Bastet's early days she was worshipped in Bubastis in Egypt's Nile Delta, where she was a formidable lioness-like goddess who would paw angrily at the sun. It took 2,000 years before she was able to upgrade her reputation and was depicted as a peaceful, slightly *vanilla*, domestic cat or cat-headed woman with maternal magic and a lithe, feline body; the first Furry, if you will.

In ancient Egypt cats were intrinsic to a successful everyday life. When not dozing in the African sun, they spent their days hunting mice, rats and snakes. No wonder they were revered! Thousands of them were mummified and preserved for the afterlife – and with the ancient Egyptians' penchant for campery, it is thought royal cats were dressed up dripping in gold and jewels.

As daughter of the sun god, Ra, Bastet was given a protector role, watching over her father as he performed his sun-pulling duties, and even slaying the chaos serpent Apep, her father's greatest enemy, in a bloody, *kaiju*-style monster mash. But more common perceptions of Bastet are a little less violent. To some, she is the Lady of the East, the Goddess of the Rising Sun, and the Sacred and All-Seeing Eye. And, for some, she is even thought of as the Goddess of the Moon. What is fascinating is the enduring power of Bastet: she survived thousands of years of history and conflict with her fame intact, and she is still worshipped today. In fact, every time you scritch behind your cat's ear, Bastet's whiskers tingle.

THE CHESHIRE CAT

THE GRINNING LITERARY CREATION

BRITISH
SHORTHAIR

To *Wonderland*, or rather, *Alice's Adventures in Wonderland*, the 1865 children's classic by Lewis Carroll, and its feline star, the Cheshire Cat. Carroll's novel (and its sequel, *Alice Through the Looking Glass*, 1871) were playful, nonsensical tales inspired by Carroll's nieces, the Liddell girls – and Alice, in particular. The two books are peppered with puns, rhymes and odd animal characters, and the green-eyed Cheshire Cat is perhaps the oddest: he has the habit of shape-shifting and disappearing, with only his disembodied grin remaining. In the upside world of *Wonderland*, the Cheshire Cat is the only character who listens to Alice; he's her guide, although an intentionally confusing one at that. "'But I don't want to go among mad people,' says Alice to the cat. 'Oh, you can't help that,' said the Cat. 'We're all mad here. I'm mad. You're mad.'"

Alice's Adventures was not the Cheshire Cat's debut; he had been an English folk-myth long before Carroll's literary creation. He first appeared in the late 1700s in Francis Grose's infamous *A Classical Dictionary of the Vulgar Tongue*, where he is listed as inspiring the saying "He grins like a Cheshire cat", which apparently was "said of anyone who shows his teeth and gums in laughing". But Carroll's inspiration may have come from old carvings of cats on a 16th-century church tower in Carroll's native Cheshire and at nearby Brimstage Hall . . . or even a wedge of delicious cheese, as it is thought a type of

Cheshire cheese moulded into the form of a grinning cat might also have been a source of inspiration for Carroll.

There are many endearing pop culture versions of the Cheshire Cat, and each underlines the hallmarks of feline behaviour: playfulness, self-involvement, and mystery. Disney's masterful animated adaptation, *Alice in Wonderland* (1951), has him plump and mischievous, ringed in lurid pink stripes; in Tim Burton's live action version (2010) he's a smoky grey tabby with a kittenish face and the soporific drawl of Stephen Fry. The original woodcut illustrations by *Punch* cartoonist Sir John Tenniel are of a grinning Cheshire Cat, much larger than Alice, hunched malevolently in a tree. Personally commissioned by Carroll, Tenniel's originals are the cat's whiskers.

THE CHESHIRE CAT

THE CHESHIRE CAT

THE DEMON CAT OF WASHINGTON, DC

EVEN SCARIER THAN YOUR AVERAGE POLITICIAN

The iconic US Capitol Building on the eastern end of the Mall in Washington, DC, is a 19th-century neoclassical confection, all columns and statues and secret passages set under a glistening dome; it's a palace to US democracy. The meeting place of the US Congress, it was infamously attacked by citizens in 2021 and was all but destroyed in *Mars Attacks*, *Independence Day* and *The Day After Tomorrow*. But you may not know that it is also the stalking ground of a ghostly feline known as the Demon Cat.

Tales of a spectral "doom cat" padding through the halls of the Capitol Building have been around for as long as the building itself. The overarching legend is that a nightwatchman discovered a small black cat stalking the halls of the building, watching aghast as it swelled to a tiger-sized, monstrous feline that attacked him before vanishing into thin air. Other tall tales suggest those who saw the Demon Cat die of fright, or that its presence foretells national tragedies.

The media was enthralled. The

Demon Cat was a "truly horrific apparition", reported the *Washington Post* in 1898, that could "swell up to the size of an elephant", and in 1935 it published the story of a Capitol guard who had seem the Demon Cat, describing how it "hissed like a washboiler" and jumped with its "teeth agleam".

Demon Cat diehards point to the evidence: paw prints in the concrete slabs of the Small Senate Rotunda and more outside the old Supreme Court Chamber. But historians roll their eyes at such stories, pointing out the laidback drinking culture of the original nightwatchmen, and how the paw prints are more likely to have been the work of vermin-hunting cats rather than a demonic feline presence.

GHOST

REX & HIS FELINE FRIENDS

THE CATS WHO RAN THE MUSEUM

VARIOUS

In the 1960s, the British Museum in Fitzrovia, London, noticed a new, somewhat unexpected exhibit had appeared in its hallowed halls: a pack of stray cats. The British Museum is old – very old. Founded in 1759, it predates the Industrial Revolution and is home to ancient Egyptian artifacts, sublime Islamic arts and countless plundered antiquities. With endless galleries, halls and staff-only shortcuts, there are many, many places in which a clever cat can hide.

In the shadows, museum cats feasted on mice and discarded snacks from visitors, and they naturally grew in numbers for close to 15 years. Kittens would scamper along the library shelves and poop in mysterious places, and, at one point, their numbers were close to a startling 100. The novelty of housing a slightly smelly cat colony eventually wore thin and staff set about humanely whittling the population.

But with the welfare of cats in question, a feline hero emerged. That hero was museum cleaner and full-time cat-lover Rex Shepherd. The British Museum was already known in the cat-world for being feline-friendly and had enjoyed the protection of a cat named Mike, who guarded the museum gates in the early 1900s. Knowing the museum was predisposed to care for cats, Rex had an idea. Also known as "the cat man", Rex soon formed The British Museum Cat Welfare Society, and for the next two decades, Rex and Society volunteers kept the colony well-cared for with neutering, spaying and an insistence on a healthy environment for their feline friends.

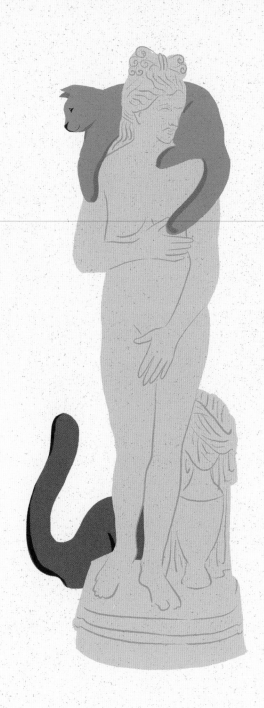

REX & HIS FELINE FRIENDS

The colony repaid Rex and the museum with kindness and column inches. Newspaper clippings from the '80s and '90s feature Suzie, who could catch a pigeon mid-flight (earning her a mention in the *New York Times*), comic cat duo Pippin & Poppin and dear little Wilson (named after Sir David Wilson, the museum's then director and definitely *not* a cat-lover). Eventually, the celeb cats became a tourist attraction themselves until, after years of de-sexing, they too disappeared into the great cat archive in the sky. But a sign from this time still hangs at the museum, just off stage. Reading, "It is strictly forbidden to feed cats in this area. The authorised feed place is . . . by the builders' skip", it is an officious reminder of when the cats ran the museum.

BIG-BONED TIBS

THE FIRST POST OFFICE CAT EMPLOYEE

MOGGY

Let's turn to London, 1964, and the Post Office's affectionate obituary for one of their most diligent and successful employees. Tibs, an imposing, Henry VIII of a cat, had sadly passed away, but – as printed in a feature in *Post Office Magazine* – he left behind a lifetime of arduous, dedicated lazing. He reigned over the staff refreshment lounge of the old Post Office headquarters in St Martin's Le Grand, growing chunky on rats and scraps; it took two men to remove Tibs' regal frame and carry him to his final resting place.

An official Post Office employee for 14 years, Tibs had enjoyed a wage of two shillings and sixpence per week to maintain the rat-free status of the HQ (he had eradicated the rat population early in his career). He was such a fixture, Tibs was only known to have left the Post Office HQ twice in his life: once for simple medical treatment, and the other to attend a celebrity cat party (or so *Post Office Magazine* claims).

Tibs, however, wasn't the first Post Office feline employee. In the 1860s there were three paid mousers scampering about the Money Order Office. They were on one shilling a week (which went towards their room and board) and sailed through their six-month probation. And Tibs wasn't the last Post Office cat either; another official feline served at the HQ until 1984.

A UNIQUE POSTAL SERVICE

MEET THE WORST DELIVERY CATS IN THE WORLD

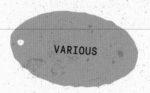

VARIOUS

Back to the 1870s, when cat intelligence was finally being recognised – and celebrated. The Belgians, clearly a cat-loving people, had realised the incredible prowess of the domestic cat and undertook an audacious experiment set to transform the lives of ordinary Belgians, and their cats, forever.

Enter the Belgian Society for the Elevation of the Domestic Cat and their extraordinary plan: to harness the natural sense of direction of the average cat by giving them jobs delivering mail. A group of 37 cats were rounded up from villages near Liege and press-ganged into delivering mail which had been put into small bags attached to their collars. They were set free with the understanding they would soon return home, thereby delivering mail to their owners, thanks to their near-magical natural navigation system.

Obviously, the fantastical story made the papers. In 1879 the *Intelligencer Journal* of Lancaster, PA, reported that the Belgians had created a society for the "mental and moral improvement" of cats, and that "carrier pigeons will have to look out for their laurels". And the *Chicago Inter Ocean* was also impressed, reporting on the "ingenious Belgians" and their potentially world-changing idea.

The cats, of course, had other ideas. They gambolled about, played in the fields, licked at their nether regions and generally did anything but return home in a timely fashion. Although all the cats turned up eventually, with the notes intact, they had no sense of urgency whatsoever and the experiment was deemed a failure. It seems if you place any expectation on a feline, you will be disappointed.

NALA

THE CAT WHO TRAVELLED THE WORLD

Imagine meeting the man of your dreams (a handsome, thick-thighed one-time rugby player, no less), falling instantly in love and setting off together to explore the world. Luckily for Nala, the subject of bestselling biography *Nala's World*, she doesn't have to imagine. For her, it's really happening.

The hunky man in question is Dean Nicholson, a Scot who left his job as a welder and decided to cycle across the world with burly best friend Ricky. After leaving Dunbar, East Lothian, in 2018, their first stop was Amsterdam, then Belgium, Greece, Switzerland and Italy, with Dean broadcasting their travels and travails on Instagram. Three months in, Ricky returned to Scotland, but Dean travelled on, his journey of self-discovery not yet over (think *Eat, Pray, Love* but with lycra and chafing). And it was in Bosnia that Dean's life truly changed.

Approaching the border to Montenegro, cycling up a big hill, Dean heard a "wee cat miaowing from behind" him. It was a small kitten – a marmalade tabby with green eyes – and she would not leave Dean alone, sprinting after him as he cycled along. He stopped and settled her on the front of his bike, intending to check her microchip details at the next town. Nala crawled from the front of his bike onto his shoulder, nestling into his neck – an unbelievably cute move. He called her Nala.

Nala had no microchip. "I just thought that was it," Dean told the BBC. "She was coming with me on this tour." And that is just what happened. Dean and Nala decided to travel the world together – by bike, of course – with Nala riding on Dean's shoulders, just as she had the first day they met.

With more than 800,000 Instagram followers, 10,000 miles travelled and the publication of *Nala's World*, the pair are enjoying their popularity, staying with friends and fans across the world. And while Dean has been introduced to the bureaucracy of pet travel, like the delays and the waiting around, Nala has taught him to enjoy the moment, to connect with others and be open-hearted to the little roadside surprises that life offers you.

BOB

THE CAT WHO TRANSFORMED A MAN'S LIFE

MOGGY

Meet James Bowen: British musician, author and special cat envoy. As a self-described "tearaway kid", Bowen's early life was fraught with difficulty. As a young man in London, his dreams of forming a band fell apart and he started sleeping in shelters or on the streets; it was a hugely precarious situation to be in, and he started to use heroin. One day he found a thin, patchy-coated but handsome marmalade tabby in the hallway of his temporary accommodation. The cat was claimed by no one and, having spent his last £20 on antibiotics from Islington's famous Blue Cross vet van, James and the cat – now named Bob – developed an affinity. James was now responsible for Bob, and his life began to change.

The pair became inseparable, with Bob travelling on the no. 73 bus with James to and from London's famous Covent Garden, where he would busk and sell street newspaper *The Big Issue*. At the same time, James enrolled on a methadone programme. The pair became well known, with fans posting videos of them, and others started travelling to Covent Garden to see them, and soon they were in the local press. A book deal followed, and James and Bob became something of a brand – James's story and his love of Bob captured the hearts of anyone who would listen. James's books (*A Street Cat Named Bob*, *The World According to Bob* and *A Gift from Bob*) are international bestsellers, and the pair took promotional trips to Norway, Germany, France, Belgium, Portugal and even Japan. Their story also inspired two British feature films (*A Street Cat Named Bob*, 2016, and *A Gift from Bob*, 2020).

Bob passed away in 2020, but in 2021 a memorial to the famous cat was installed on Islington Green, a small city park in London near the spot where James and Bob first met, to mark the charitable work Bob inspired in James and countless others.

SNOW WHITE

THE START OF HEMINGWAY'S FELINE OBSESSION

Everyone knows Ernest Hemingway as the iconic Nobel-winning American author of *For Whom the Bell Tolls* and renowned cocktail lover (he loved a mojito). Hemingway's life was lived in full colour: he travelled the world, rubbed shoulders with other great writers, safari-ed, served in the First World War, fought in the Spanish Civil War and enjoyed numerous marriages. But you might not know that he was also a six-toed cat fancier.

While in Paris he wrote that he was "too poor to even own a cat", but during his years in Cuba and the island of Key West, Florida, Hemingway become a true cat person. In 1935 local mariner Captain Stanley Dexter gave the writer a white six-toed Maine Coon kitten, also known as a polydactyl, called Snowball. Hemingway's sons renamed her Snow White, and from there his cat collection grew, with many named after a storybook character or celebrity. There was Willard Scott, Errol Flynn and

little Gremlin, who lived for 19 years. But there were others, too: Friendless, Feather Kitty and Uncle Woofer. At his house, Finca Vigía in Cuba, he was thought to have had over 50 cats hopping on and off the dining table and snuggling in guests' beds. In 1943 he wrote from Cuba to his wife: "One cat just leads to another . . . The place is so damned big it doesn't really seem as though there were many cats until you see them all moving like a mass migration at feeding time." In Key West, his cat colony grew further. At Key West's Ernest Hemingway Home and Museum, some of the descendants of the great writer's original feline smorgasbord still roam the estate, most with more than the average number of toes (just how Hemingway liked them).

It seems Hemingway drew inspiration from his cat pack. "No animal has more liberty than the cat," he wrote, "but it buries the mess it makes. The cat is the best anarchist."

OCELOT

BABOU

SALVADOR DALÍ'S LITTLE HELLRAISER

Salvador Dalí (1904–1989), the eccentric and moustachioed Spanish surrealist and art school dropout, left Madrid in 1926 for Paris, where he met Miró and Picasso and cultivated his celebrity artist status. By 1936 he was on the cover of *TIME* magazine and went on to paint celebrities like Coco Chanel and Sigmund Freud, and he even appeared in adverts. His brash publicity stunts and shock-value outfits saw Dalí fall out with the staid art establishment, but there was one thing in his life he never turned his back on: his love of cats.

Cats had always been in Dalí's life, but it was in 1960, when Dalí lived in New York City, that he was introduced to his true love: an ocelot (a large, part-domesticated wild cat also known as a dwarf leopard) called Babou, given to him by the Colombian head of state – or so the legend goes. Babou lived a life of incredible luxury, from his stone-studded collar to luxury cruises. Writer and celebrity astrologer Suzanne White described seeing the cat padding about "on a silken settee located in front of a carved marble fireplace" in Dalí's apartment. And there was a fateful trip to a swanky Manhattan restaurant: led into the fashionable eatery on a leash, the cheetah-like cat slipped free only to thrill and frighten the other diners. Spanish actor Carlos Lozano, an eyewitness, said he "only saw the ocelot smile once: the day it escaped and sent the guests at the Meurice scurrying like rats for cover".

One of Dalí's most celebrated surrealist works is a piece with photographer Philippe Halsman in which a trio of cats take to the air in a sort of live action version of Dalí's paintings. In the photograph, columns of water, furniture, Dalí himself and his cat models are weightless yet poised for action. The production of the shoot was not quite so delicately rendered, with assistants merely chucking the cats into the air before Dalí jumped – giving the effect of the artist and his felines having the power of flight. The end of Babou and Dalí's flying cats is unknown, but it is clear they were an integral part of the artist's work.

HOMER

THE BLIND CRIME-FIGHTING WONDER CAT

So often, the story of a fantastical cat reveals something of the human who cares for it. The bond between cat and human – utterly unique, full of thrilling tension – relies on the human to be, at the very least, caring, but it sometimes requires the complete emotional upheaval of one's life. So it was with Homer, a black sightless cat, and his human, Gwen Cooper. Homer, blind from three weeks old, was given to Cooper in 1997, who later wrote: "Fate may have taken Homer's eyes, but he had my heart from the moment I first held him."

At the time, Cooper was just 24 and living in a friend's spare room after a break-up. She had already acquired two cats of her own, so a third, blind cat was the last thing she needed. But it seemed Homer – named after the blind Ancient Greek writer of the *Iliad* and the *Odyssey* – would soon change her life. In 2007 her debut book, *Diary of a South Beach Party Girl*, revealed her time on the 1990s Miami party circuit, but it is arguably her feline follow-up memoir that is her most beloved work. In fact, *Homer's Odyssey: A Fearless Feline Tale, or How I Learned about Love and Life with a Blind Wonder Cat* (2009) is a *New York Times* bestseller and has been published in 22 languages. Detailing Cooper and Homer's life together, the memoir deals in the misadventures of Homer, his pack-mates Vashti and Scarlett, and Cooper herself as she hot-stepped through her own turbulent times. She tells of Homer sizing up an armed robber who attempted to burgle her Miami apartment, and in another chapter Cooper describes her travails in returning home to Homer, Vashti and Scarlett, who were trapped alone together in an apartment near the World Trade Center after 9/11. During his lifetime, Homer – and the other cats – became the centre of Cooper's world, a gravitational pull of responsibility that helped Cooper learn some essential life skills.

Homer went on to inspire several books and, through their story together, Cooper has been able to raise awareness of "special needs" cats (who are often first on the list to be euthanised in cat shelters) and the richness they can bring to a human's life. As Cooper writes: "Love is love, whether it goes on two legs or four."

CREME PUFF

THE WORLD'S OLDEST CAT

From Oscar Wilde's *The Picture of Dorian Gray* to cinematic classic *Death Becomes Her*, the secret of immortality has long bewitched and befuddled the human race, but to no avail. It took a cat named Creme Puff and her owner, a Texan plumber named Jake Perry, to start to decipher the spell.

Born in 1967, Creme Puff was a more-than-average domestic cat, who – incredibly – lived for more than three decades. She was the world's longest-living cat, notching up 38 years and three days (that's 168 in cat years) before passing away in 2005, a feat only narrowly missed by another of Perry's cats, Grandpa Rex Allen. Verified by the Guinness Book of Records, the pair, and their many adoptive brothers and sisters, are local legends in Austin, and with cat-lovers around the world.

Creme Puff's science-defying fame tends to eclipse the tireless work of her human, Jake Perry, who devoted his life to adopting and re-homing hundreds of cats. At one time he cared for more than 40 felines at his residential home, which was retro-fitted with cat runs. And it wasn't just Creme Puff and

Grandpa who nearly lived forever – Perry claimed that around a third of his cats lived to at least 30 years old.

Much has been made of Perry's longevity techniques, but one thing is for sure: almost all of them are unorthodox. Apart from dry cat food jazzed up with broccoli, eggs and turkey bacon, he also fed Creme and the other cats coffee with cream, the occasional pipette of red wine, and played the pack nature documentaries (sometimes in 3D, requiring the cats to wear glasses . . . or so the legend goes). The cats were also treated to Easter baskets, turkey dinners at Thanksgiving and Champagne and party hats on New Year's Eve.

In the end, the secret to Creme Puff's near-immortality seems almost obvious, and possible for the average human too. Perhaps all of us might live to 168 if we followed Creme's lead. Clearly there's something to be said for good food, great TV, hanging out with friends, alcohol in moderation and party hats when the occasion suits.

GRUMPY CAT

THE FIRST INTERNET CATFLUENCER

The internet – the wellspring of cat pictures, memes and mishaps – has helped lend fame to an almost infinite number of feline wannabes. Thankfully, the talent bar is high: these aren't just cats that chase their own tail or drink from a glass but rather excel in their chosen art. They might ride goats, fight bears or deftly knock precious ornaments from shelves when the owner is watching. For all these best-in-show cats, it might be argued there is one who was a true pioneer of the internet age. That cat is Tardar Sauce, also known as Grumpy Cat.

Tardar, born in Arizona in 2012, was a simple calico and tabby cross with an underbite, feline dwarfism and an accidentally grumpy look that belied her cheery disposition: catty resting face, if you will. Although her unique look was fascinating, Tardar was destined to live the simple life of a much-loved house cat with her human, Tabatha Bundesen. That is until Tardar's photo found its way onto Reddit and, almost overnight, a million memes of the world's grumpiest-looking cat were born. From then on, Grumpy Cat was a brand. She quickly accepted representation by a meme manager and worked hard to underpin her fame. Within a year, Tabatha left her job to manage Tardar's TV appearances and ad campaigns. Then came a book, a movie (with Tardar voiced by actor Aubrey Plaza), a trip to South by Southwest festival in Austin and a number of meme awards (make of that what you will). And at one point, there were more than 1,000 items of grumpy merch (including tees, calendars, swimwear, a fragrance and more) available, and a craze of Grumpy Cat tattoos. Tardar's entourage worked hard to protect her brand, winning a lawsuit for breach of contract with a collaborator.

But what of Tardar herself? Luckily, her grumpy persona was just an act, a little showbiz for the cameras, and in her private life she was well adjusted and well loved. Tardar passed away in 2019 at a rather young age, but – like all memes – her legacy lives on: the grumpy cat who made others smile.

CALICO-TABBY
CROSS

MRS CHIPPY

THE CAT WHO (ALMOST) ESCAPED
SHACKLETON'S DOOMED EXPEDITION

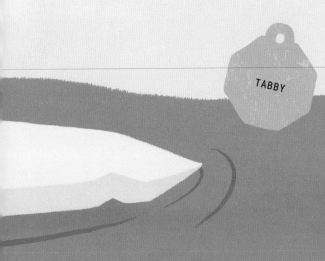

TABBY

In 2022 a group of historian-explorers discovered the wreck of a ship in the depths of the Weddell Sea, crushed by sea ice 107 years before. It was *Endurance*, Sir Ernest Shackleton's infamous vessel aboard which he and 27 others undertook his Trans-Antarctic Expedition in 1914. Miraculously, when *Endurance* became trapped in pack ice, Shackleton and the others all survived, but there was one honorary crew member who sadly perished: Mrs Chippy, the ship's cat, a delightfully characterful Scottish tabby.

Mrs Chippy was the devoted cat of the ship's carpenter, Harry "Chippy" McNish, and was named by the crew to honour the feline's obsession with McNish (no matter the cat was male). Mrs Chippy had the run of the ship, catching mice and rats, dancing coquettishly on the dogs' kennels and even climbing the rigging. The captain, Frank Worsley, described this feat as "exactly after the manner of a seaman going aloft". Mrs Chippy survived several near-death experiences, including falling overboard, and was adored by the crew, who were impressed by his sea-legs (he could pad along inch-wide rails in the roughest waters).

When *Endurance* became stuck in the ice and the decision was made to abandon ship, with the crew escaping on foot across the ice, a horrifying choice had to be made. Knowing Mrs Chippy and some of the dogs might not survive the perilous escape, it was decided the dependent animals would be euthanised. McNish and the dog handlers were utterly distraught, and it is said the carpenter never forgave Shackleton. But the men went on to survive, in large part thanks to McNish's refitting of a single lifeboat that helped the men travel 800 miles to safety.

Years later, the memory of Mrs Chippy loomed large in the hearts and minds of the crew. McNish continued to tell all who would listen that "Shackleton killed my cat", and passed away in New Zealand in 1930 all but forgotten and without the Polar Medal the rest of the *Endurance* crew received. In 2004 the New Zealand Antarctic Society renovated McNish's grave in Karori Cemetery, Wellington, celebrating McNish's life and reuniting man and cat. A bronze statue of Mrs Chippy now sprawls across his human's tomb, the pair now together forever.

FANNY

THE PETA-ENDORSED, INDIE-DARLING COVER GIRL

In 2010, a million years ago in the digital age, British photographer Jake Walters took on a new portrait commission for the *Guardian*. The subject? The Smith's frontman and Northern-English indie-crooner Morrissey. At the time, the pair had been friends for two decades and, with the help of Walters' young Bengal named Fanny, they accidentally created one of the most iconic photographs of the musician, with the cat taking centre stage.

When Fanny met Morrissey "it was love at first sight", Walters told Another.com. "I didn't even get a look in." And it was Morrissey who was keen to do a shot with Fanny. "I can't remember who came up with the idea of sitting her on his head," said Walters, "but because it's Morrissey, I'll give the credit to him." Perched resplendently on the "Girlfriend in a Coma" singer's head like a crown, Fanny stole the show.

Two years later, US animal rights organisation PETA acquired the photo, audaciously using it in their own media, posing the question, "What's on Morrissey's Mind? Animal Overpopulation".

Among the many subjects Morrissey has spoken out about – some more gentle on the ears than others – animal rights is one of his enduring and most-heartfelt issues. The singer has been a vegetarian since The Smiths' *Meat is Murder* album release in 1985. As barbarism begins at home, there is little doubt Fanny's starring role helped push PETA's spaying and neutering campaign, with the organisation focused on lowering the millions of unwanted cats euthanised each year.

It makes sense it was a Bengal that changed the fortunes of the unwanted cats of the US. The breed, a cross between the spotted Egyptian Mau and the Asian leopard cat, is particularly powerful and, although some girls are bigger than others, Fanny was young and slim in her iconic portrait and soon grew to typical Bengal athleticism. The regal-looking breed has a confident, Bengal-knows-best attitude, and thanks to Walters, Morrissey and Fanny, we can only imagine how many unwanted cats have been saved.

TOWSER THE MOUSER

THE MOST MURDEROUS CAT IN THE WORLD

MOGGY

As every cat-lover knows, even the cutest, most placid felines tend to have a jaw-dropping murderous streak; cats and high mouse-mortality rates fit together like paw in hand. And the most insatiable, most cut-throat cat of them all was Towser (1963–1987), a Scottish-born long-haired grey tortoiseshell with a chillingly long and record-breaking kill-list.

Towser's domain was the Glenturret Distillery in Crieff,

overlooking the River Turret, an ancient whisky-maker creating the world's most delicious liquor since the 1700s. Whisky production requires the storing of high-grade barley, and Towser's job was to patrol the barley stores to gently dissuade mice against nibbling the grain. Towser excelled at her job and her kill-rate was a comfortable three mice a day. She did this without fail for almost her whole 24 years, notching up an incredible

28,899 mice. News of Towser, a local legend among distillery workers, soon reached the Guinness Book of Records, who sent a representative to observe her over several days (working out the approximate figures for her almost unbelievable success rate).

Glenturret remains a cat-friendly distillery, with feline and human working together to produce their delicious whisky. Although there has been a succession of Towser replacements, all beloved by the Glenturret crew, none have surpassed her incredible reign. There is even a bronze statue onsite in her honour. Who knows what powered Towser's prowess towards murder? Perhaps she was born with the ability to behead mice with a single snap of her jaws, or perhaps it was the drop of whisky added to her milk every night? Nature or nurture, Towser was the world's most skilful and faithful mouse-killer.

GLI

THE UNDISPUTED QUEEN OF THE HAGIA SOPHIA

EUROPEAN
SHORTHAIR

Those lucky enough to enter the glittering Hagia Sophia in Istanbul are transported back hundreds of years to the Byzantine world. The immense building – a feat of artistry and engineering dating back to 500AD that became the religious and political centre of the world – overflows with art and mosaics and was once the cultural core of the Byzantine era. The Sophia's incarnations are many, from Christian to Greek Orthodox to the site of Muslim worship after the conquering of Constantinople (Istanbul) in 1453, after which the site was studded with four soaring minarets. Although still an official site of worship, the Hagia Sophia's grandiose structure has a regal feel which serves as catnip to cats, and there was one cat of note who reigned over its hallowed halls.

All hail Gli (2004–2020), the unofficial queen of the Hagia Sophia and a delightful European shorthair with shimmering green, sweetly crossed eyes, a rather regal countenance and a penchant for posing perfectly in countless tourist photos. Gli was born at the Hagia Sophia with her two siblings, Kizim and Pati, and the three had the run of the building (a museum at the time). Of course, it was Gli who shone out and she soon became a hit with visitors. She met dignitaries like President Obama and the Turkish President and soon joined Instagram, deftly rising to fame.

Cats feature in many ancient faith stories and take on several starring roles in traditional Islamic tales, so there was some synchronicity in Gli's hallowed role at the Hagia Sophia, and news of her demise in 2020 was heard around the world. But her story doesn't end there: the Instagram account inspired by Gli now boasts more than 100,000 followers, and tourists and worshippers still flock to Hagia Sophia to be awestruck by its beauty, feel closer to their own beliefs and perhaps catch a glimpse of Gli's multitude of cat descendants.

HAMLET

THE ACTORS' CAT OF THE ALGONQUIN HOTEL

Let's check in to the Algonquin on West 44th Street, New York City's most lauded and luxurious hotel, with a long-held penchant for feline guests. Apart from being Manhattan's most arguably pet-friendly palace, the Algonquin has long employed a rather special cat as its official, full-time mascot.

The story, steeped in myth and lore, began almost a century ago when screen legend John Barrymore was resident at the hotel. In the 1920s – the era of the famed Algonquin round table and the snarky celeb writers, artists and woeful wits who would hold court there – the hotel was also famous for Billy, a marmalade tabby who sauntered into the lobby and stayed there. He soon had free rein of the hotel and, when he passed away, another cat wandered in to take his place. In 1932 Barrymore, in a fit of theatrics, suggested a new name, Hamlet, to honour his most beloved Shakespearean role. There are even tales of Billy (or might it be Hamlet?) lapping milk from a Champagne glass. A legend was born and, decade after decade, the Algonquin has replaced each dear departed or retired Hamlet with another rescue cat happy to take on the mantle. The Algonquin's infamous Hamlets – and their female counterparts, always called Matilda – are much-loved. There's now a full-time human-held chief cat officer position at the hotel, cat access doors and cat trees, and the door staff love to keep the hotel cats amused.

Thankfully the Algonquin's feline-focus doesn't stop here: there are cat reiki sessions (of course), official merch, Hamlet and Matilda books, an email account where you can send Hamlet or Matilda a message, and endless photo opportunities with guests. Knowing all this feline fuss translates into dollars, the Algonquin is keen to give back and holds an annual summer fund raiser for the Mayor's Alliance for NYC's Animals, a network of 150 animal shelters, during which Hamlet headlines a cat fashion show. Today you'll find the current Hamlet or Matilda at the front desk, napping, or coquettishly allowing themself the luxury of strokes from excitable guests.

BLACKIE

THE RICHEST CAT IN THE WORLD

MOGGY

As we depart this world for the great kitty litter tray in the sky, we might consider leaving our wealth and possessions to our most beloved – the one who has been with us through the good times and the bad, the one with whom we have an unbreakable, forever-bond. And for more people than one might imagine, this loved one can sometimes be a cat. Meet Blackie, named the world's richest cat in 2011 and the recipient of a whisker-twitching fortune in her late owner's will.

When antiquities collector Ben Rea sadly passed away in 1988, he left most of his immense fortune – in the millions – to his beloved black cat. At one time, Rea lived happily with 14 cats, and Blackie was the final surviving feline of the family, outliving Rea and all her own relatives. Animal charities, who received the rest of the fund, were tasked with caring for Blackie in accordance with Rea's final wishes.

Of course, Blackie isn't the only animal to be bequeathed a fortune, and differing reports suggest another cat is even richer than Blackie. On the streets of Rome prowled Tommaso, a stray cat who sauntered into the life of one Maria Assunta, whose personal fortune stretched into the millions. Unable to find the right organisation to take on her beloved stray once she passed away, Assunta created a trust and Tommaso became its sole recipient, inheriting the 94-year-old's property portfolio when she died in 2011.

Cynical cat people might suspect foul play, pointing out the unlikely happenstance of a cat wandering into an aging millionaire's life just at the right moment, but whether Blackie or Tommaso top the cat rich list, there can be no doubt of the undying love they inspired in their owners.

HODGE

THE CAT WHO INSPIRED THE DICTIONARY

Infamous writer and *bon vivant* Samuel Johnson ruled the British literary scene of 1700s. A towering hulk of a man, he wrote moving plays, delicate poetry and spellbinding novels, and was also an editor, critic and dictionary maker; his work forming the basis of modern literary criticism. Although the brawny word-wrestler – also known as Dr Johnson – drew inspiration from many sources, it is thought his true muse was his menagerie of cats . . . and a cute little furball affectionately named Hodge in particular.

Hodge the cat ruled Johnson's London residence in Gough Square and is commemorated there in the form of a small bronze by Jon Bickley. The statue depicts Hodge sitting on a dictionary (arguably Johnson's most important work) with a small stack of oyster shells, a nod to Johnson's habit of treating his cat with delicious morsels. In a time where one's lowly service staff would do literally anything for you, Johnson would buy Hodge oysters himself, apparently so the staff wouldn't resent the love the writer showered on his cat. And in Hodge's later years, Johnson would buy him valerian to cure his ills. The fact that Dr Johnson had uncontrollable tics has led some to ponder if the genius was neurodivergent, and it is thought his cats helped calm and focus his mind. Would we have the dictionary as we know it without Johnson? Definitely. But would he have created it without the camaraderie he so clearly enjoyed with Hodge? Who is to say?

Contemporaries of Johnson would mention Hodge in their pen portraits of the man, and later biographers have also weighed in on his feline obsessions. In Scottish biographer James Boswell's *Life of Johnson*, he writes, "I recollect him one day scrambling up Dr Johnson's breast, apparently with much satisfaction, while my friend smiling and half-whistling, rubbed down his back, and pulled him by the tail." If this isn't a description of true human-feline love, then what is?

CAT CORLEONE

THE REAL POWER BEHIND COPPOLA'S *THE GODFATHER*

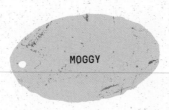

MOGGY

Film freaks love nothing more than to devour a scene of their favourite movie, chewing over the blocking, lighting, performances, costume design and *mise en scene*, hoping to swallow down the film's true hidden meaning. One theory concerns Francis Ford Coppola's mafia classic *The Godfather* and claims the true power of this seemingly patriarchal family rests not with Marlon Brando's Don Vito Corleone, but rather a tiny black-and-white stray cat.

The famous cat was a stray Coppola discovered on the Paramount lot, and it was the director himself who plonked it, unscripted, into the great actor's lap during the filming of the iconic early scene. "The cat in Marlon's hands was not planned for," Coppola once told *Time*. "I saw the cat running around the studio and took it and put it in his hands without a word." Knowing Brando was an animal lover, it was a gamble he was willing to take. In the movie, Corleone strokes the cat while deciding who should live and who should die, and the cat clearly loved its proximity to Brando's nether regions, as it purred so loudly it eclipsed some of the actor's lines.

Cat fans know of the feline's preternatural ability to be in the right place at the right time, and some claim the cat manipulated the filmmakers into featuring it on screen; it was certainly a scene-stealer. But perhaps it sensed Brando was a confirmed cat person. The actor had his own feline friends and is even quoted as saying, "I live in my cat's house." But how did the cat alter the film's narrative? What meaning was Coppola trying to convey? Did the cat show Corleone's softer side, or depict the hidden, razor-sharp claws beneath his lazy, cat-in-the-sun demeanour?

SALEM

THE WISE-CRACKING WITCH'S FAMILIAR

AMERICAN
SHORTHAIR

American Archie Comics' series *Sabrina the Teenage Witch* is a cultural milestone, and the 1990s TV series it inspired is considered canon, especially by those whose own teenage years coincided with Sabrina's. As a deliciously spooky take on the family sitcom, the show featured the ups and downs of the life of young witch Sabrina Spellman and her aunts, Hilda and Zelda, in the fictional town of Greendale (near Riverdale, another magic-themed TV show). And Salem Saberhagen (voiced by writer and comedian Nick Bakay) was their cynical, wise-cracking and rather hard-done-by American Shorthair cat. Salem's first appearance in *Archie's Mad House* #22 in 1962 depicted a pumpkin-coloured feline, but fandom surrounding the '90s TV adaptation, a contemporary Netflix version, the animated series and graphic novels has forced a rethink, and Salem is now a black cat with shimmering green eyes.

Of course, cats and witches have long been co-conspirators. Historically, the cat is not just a mere companion but a creature with whom one can maintain a psychic link, with the cat acting as an avatar for its owner – something most cat people can attest to. At least, that was the thought behind the wave of

misogynistic witch trials that swept through fundamentalist religious communities in the 1600s, including the town of Salem, Massachusetts, after which Sabrina's cat is named. Women suspected of witchcraft (or rather, the victims of feuding families and their problematic children) were put to death, many along with their cats, long-considered Satanic by religious authorities. Luckily, Sabrina and Salem escaped a similar fate and live on in countless memes, merch, re-makes, Halloween outfits and Comic Con appearances. And although his acting days are mostly behind him, Salem is probably the most famous TV cat in the world. "I wasn't always the stud muffin I am today" is one of his more memorable quotes.

HESTER, SAM AND FRIENDS

ANDY WARHOL'S CAT COLONY

Andy Warhol, the bewigged superstar art king, began his career in the 1950s as a lowly freelance children's book illustrator. Those early NYC days were lean for Warhol, and his mother, Julia, also an illustrator, moved into his Lexington Avenue apartment to help share costs. They were soon joined by Hester, a female Siamese gifted to Andy by actress Gloria Swanson. The Warhols loved cats, and felines (and angels) were a recurring motif in Julia's work. Years later, Warhol's infamous drop-in and drop-out art space, The Factory, had its own resident cats, Black Lace and White Pussy, but Hester was the original.

The mother and son soon introduced a studly male cat, Sam, to the household, thinking this might delight Hester. They were right, and soon the Warhols found themselves hosting a small cat colony, naming each new kitten Sam after their father.

In 1954 they put their feline inspiration to paper and self-

VARIOUS

published a small, somewhat idiosyncratic book celebrating their cat family. Titled *25 Cats Name Sam and One Blue Pussy*, it featured Andy's lithographs (possibly created at one of Andy's "colouring parties") and Julia's calligraphy, a series of almost unbearably cute portraits of 16 (not 25) cats and a misspelled title (Julia had accidentally dropped the "d" off "Named", which Andy found charming). The books Hester and Sam inspired were hand signed and now fetch an eye-watering price at auction. Sadly, Hester died in 1957, and Andy and Julia self-published a sequel in her honour called *Holy Cats by Andy Warhol's Mother*, depicting Hester's adventures in heaven.

Cats went on to to feature in Warhol's art and, in his later years, eye-wateringly rich from the art-game, Warhol lived in a five-floor building surrounded by art ephemera, cookie jars, odd antiquities and many, many cats.

TELEMACHUS & NIETZSCHE

THE MUSICAL CATS OF THE HOLLYWOOD HILLS

TABBY

It was Jim McCrary, the towering, famed rock photographer, who captured the most iconic image of Telemachus, an image that can still be found in most music-loving homes across the world. The unassuming cat appeared on the cover of Carole King's *Tapestry* (1971) alongside a pared-back, sun-lit image of the legendary singer-songwriter, carefree and barefoot, and the album went on to sell an incredible 25 million copies. King's not-so-difficult second album is her most beloved, making Telemachus "perhaps the most famous tabby cat on Earth", as King herself has said.

By the time McCrary took the image, King had been in the music industry for a decade but was in the midst of a creative sea-change, turning from writer to singer-songwriter. She moved to the Hollywood Hills with her daughters, got in touch with her spiritual side and created *Tapestry*. Telemachus was clearly an essential part of her renewal and was therefore plonked, pride of place, on the cover. Cat-lovers know what an inspiration a cat can bring, and we might never have had *Tapestry* without Telemachus.

A few miles away, another cat rivalled Telemachus for empowering legendary singer-songwriters: meet Nietzsche and his human, Joni Mitchell, resplendent on the cover of her 1997 album *Taming the Tiger*. Writer Bill Flanagan asked Mitchell about the image – a self-portrait

TELEMACHUS & NIETZSCHE

in oils – in *Vanity Fair* (1997). He noted how the painting, a work in progress, developed over two visits to Mitchell's home in the Hollywood Hills and soon became the cover of *Taming*. "In the new version," wrote Flanagan, "Mitchell's hat and shirt were lighter colours, the sky behind her was a brighter blue . . . Maybe good fortune had started to sink in. 'I think this is the album cover', she said." At times, Mitchell has described the feline in the portrait as El Café, her other beloved feline muse, but whichever cat it is, it seems Mitchell drew on that peculiar type of cat energy to inform both her art and music.

Many musical greats have decamped to the Hollywood Hills and created their finest works, but it seems Telemachus and Nietzsche, two inspirational, muse-like felines, have left their paw prints on our most adored music.

FREDDIE PURRCURY & GEORGE MEOWCHAEL

THE CATS WHO ALMOST NEVER WERE

MOGGY

In 2017 a rollercoaster story of hope, loss and redemption broke cat-internet, the feline-focused, hair-balled epicentre of our digital world. It began when British actor, writer and confirmed cat-lover Alex Andreou took to Twitter to report an incident of anti-gay behaviour. The story started plaintively: "So, I just travelled two hours to adopt a cat that desperately needed re-homing and was turned down for being gay. WTF is wrong with people," wrote Andreou. "So now I'm on the bus and I'm sobbing and people are staring at me because the truth is it hurts as much as when I was eight years old."

Andreou answered an advert to care for a pair of too-cute-to-be-true rescue cats and soon found himself in an odd text message exchange on the way to collect them. The cats' owner asked: "How comes youre [sic] single, are you gay?" When Alex confirmed he was, the owner responded: "I am religious so I strongly disagree with the lifestyle. I'm sorry if I hurt your feelings." With two cats' lives at stake, Alex had a punchy response: "Darling, I've been beaten and called a 'faggot' since I was eight. My feelings are quite robust. And yes, sorry is precisely

what you are." The owner replied: "Are you not afraid of going to hell when you die?"

The response from the cat-internet was one of shock, solidarity and offers of help. In the end, Alex's friend Lisa offered to pick up the cats, but then the tale took an unexpected twist. The cat owner backed out yet again, and Alex began to wonder if the cats had ever existed at all. An online deep-dive revealed the cat ad had been up for rather a long time and the owner had backed out of placements before. And then the clincher: the photo of the cats had been lifted from another advert. The odd, anti-gay behaviour of the owner was one thing, but the question of if the cats ever existed at all will remain a mystery.

So, what of Alex's quest to care for a pair of rescue cats? After his story went viral, he was offered "all the cats", and soon after, Alex announced the end of the tale. "Here is your happy ending," he posted, alongside photos of two extremely fetching felines. The brothers, one a tawny tortoiseshell and the other black, are called George Meowchael-Andreou and Freddie Purrcury-Andreou – two wonderfully gay-edged names. And in 2022 Alex confirmed the cats are "happy and healthy and all grown up and very much the centre of our little family".

FREDDIE PURRCURY & GEORGE MEOWCHAEL

ABLE SEAMAN SIMON

THE AWARD-WINNING ROYAL NAVY CAT

MOGGY

Meet Simon, the Royal Navy's bravest cat and recipient of the Dickin Medal (the highest, most-lauded British honour awarded for animal bravery in battle). Once a scrawny black-and-white tomcat, Simon was plucked from a life on the streets of Hong Kong by a teenager, Ordinary Seaman George Hickinbottom, who was just 17 when he joined the crew of HMS *Amethyst*. He thought Simon (as George named him) would be just what the ship needed to rid it of rats and smuggled him on board, unaware of Simon's incredible bravery that was yet to be revealed.

In 1949 HMS *Amethyst* sailed up the Yangtze River from Shanghai to Nanking to relieve HMS *Consort*, which had been protecting the British embassy during China's bloody civil war. No trouble was expected but the *Amethyst* was suddenly showered with shells, with Simon horribly injured by shrapnel. Simon disappeared in the confusion and was found staggering on deck days later, near death. He was taken to the sick bay and was kept there to both recover and lift the spirits of the other survivors; many were very young men who had witnessed 20 of their crewmates die in the attack.

Surrounded by snipers, the *Amethyst* was stuck for three months in the heat and humidity, and conditions on the boat grew unbearable, with the rats seeming to take over. Thankfully, Simon, war-battled just like his brave crewmates, grew stronger every day and soon returned to his rat-catching duties. Simon caught a huge number of them, including a particularly huge rat, with the ship promoting Simon to Able Seaman. When the moment came, the *Amethyst* made its escape and sailed slowly to Hong Kong, where the ship and crew were hailed as heroes.

Simon starred in the spools of newsreel and photographs of the day, posing with his crewmates. Simon was awarded the Dickin in 1949, and in his testimonial letter to the People's Dispensary for Sick Animals, the captain wrote: "Throughout the incident Simon's behaviour was of the highest order. One would not have expected a small cat to survive the blast from an explosion capable of making a hole over a foot in diameter in a steel plate." An honorary mention should go to Peggy, the ship's dog, but it was brave Simon who stole the show.

CHARLES UTKINS

THE PSYCHIC, MIND-CONTROLLING CAT

Can a cat be haunted? Much has been made of the possible magical, supernatural abilities of certain cats, but can such a self-serving creature be possessed? Meet handsome Charles Utkins, the curiously named smoke-grey tabby at the centre of an uncanny tale that has gripped the cat-world.

The story starts in 2017, about 1,000 miles northwest of Japan in Blagoveshchensk, Russia. There, a man called Dmitry, who inherited Charles from his aunt, started to notice a series of odd feline occurrences. At first, Charles would suddenly appear from behind locked doors but soon went on to seemingly control Dmitry's dreams. "He would wake me up at 5 am," Dmitry told local media, "giving me a strong desire to eat fish or sausage." Dmitry hated fish and sausages, but Charles' powers were strong. "So much so that I had to go out right then to buy it and give it to the cat." As soon as Charles ate, Dmitry's own hunger would vanish. "He reads minds, but the worst thing – he inspires thoughts," Dmitry reported. "And these thoughts will be fulfilled; they are impossible to resist." Things at home soon turned sour, with Dmitry's wife uneasy with Charles' presence in the house, so Dmitry searched for a new owner to take on the uncanny feline.

Enter a glamorous clairvoyant from Novosibirsk in the heart of Russia, almost 3,000 miles from Blagoveshchensk. A "young, well-groomed blonde woman" is how Dmitry described her, but local media used their own shorthand: "witch". She arrived with her psychic "paraphernalia", inspected Charles and offered the couple more than £65,000 for the cat. "She deals with extrasensory phenomenon," Dmitry said. "She can see in some beings the object of her interest, and earnings. More than once she stipulated that the cat will pay off." And with that, Charles Utkins moved to Novosibirsk with the clairvoyant, pet passport in his paw. Apparently, Charles was to be used in seances, but Dmitry and his wife were just thankful to be left in psychic peace, rather well-off, and sausage-free.

SIR STUFFINGTON

ARR, HE BE THE PIRATE CAT!

MOGGY

In 2013 three tiny kittens were handed in at an animal shelter in Oregon, USA. They were all in a sorry state and one was horribly injured, with a damaged jaw, a heart murmur, fleas and a missing eye from a raccoon attack. Enter Blazer Schaffer, the Oregon-based pole-acrobat and performer who had worked with the shelter for a decade. Schaffer saw the kittens online and knew she could help. Her two children (pre-teens at the time) and girlfriend already helped foster a menagerie of animals at their home, from a blind and deaf dachshund to an iguana rescued from homelessness. Schaffer knew that the kittens – now known as Dexter, Nugget, and Sir Stuffington the one-eyed cat – would fit in perfectly.

To help find a permanent home for the cats, Schaffer posted some photos of her new brood online and, well, it's safe to say it went down rather well. The images were widely shared, picked up by popular accounts, and Sir Stuffington became a star. It was his fans who noticed a certain pirate countenance. In an interview, Schaffer told *Mother Jones* she had no idea Sir Stuffington resembled a pirate. "One day, my girlfriend sent me a bunch of emails with photos, and I saw him turned into a pirate . . . the photos on Facebook just went crazy. People said, 'Oh, my god, he's a pirate!' and it blew up from there."

From then on, Sir Stuffington was famous. His lip, curled in a permanent "arrrgh", and one-eye gave him undeniable pirate vibes, and Schaffer was quick to realise

an opportunity to advocate for animal shelters and to send out a message. "Every person can make a difference," she said to *Mother Jones*, "all you have to do is stop and pick up a stray and take him or her to a shelter or a vet." Of course, Sir Stuffington isn't the most pirate-friendly name. At first, Schaffer thought he looked like a "cute little teddy bear that lost his stuffing", but there are no plans to change his name. More important is the health of the three cats, now comfortably settled at their new owners' homes, having overcome their ill health, and are now enjoying normal cat adventures – especially Sir Stuffington, who went missing in 2014 but thankfully soon returned.

SIR STUFFINGTON

JONES

AKA BORIS, THE INTERGALACTIC ALIEN-SLAYER

TABBY

In space, no one can hear you meow. Not even if you are Boris, British comedian Sooz Kempner's childhood marmalade tabby and star of James Cameron's *Aliens*, the 1986 cult classic sci-fi movie starring Sigourney Weaver. Boris shot to stardom as Jones in Cameron's shoot-em-up sequel to Ridley Scott's original *Alien* (1979), and Kempner revealed her connection to him in her *Sooz on Film* show at the Edinburgh Festival Fringe in 2017. Although Kempner is herself hugely accomplished, she admits to being somewhat overshadowed by her cat. "Even if I achieve the ultimate dream and get an Oscar," Kempner said in an interview with writer Si Hawkins, "I'll be holding it and knowing that I'll never be as iconic as my cat."

Boris was method. He needed to hiss on command for his role as Jones, the intergalactic cat, and Kempner confirms he was just as difficult in real life as he was when on set facing up to a dripping xenomorph. "It was a particular skill-set with Boris," she said, "because he was horrible: you could get him to hiss on camera. They had another cat under cover in a cat box, and then they'd pull a blanket off it", and Boris would hiss like Sigourney's life depended on it. "You didn't need to do much to get Boris to hiss."

In *Aliens* much is made of the love affair between Sigourney Weaver's Ellen Ripley and Jones, the cryogenically frozen and thawed out ship's cat played so expertly by Boris. To promote the film, a series of playful out-of-character photographs were made of the pair cavorting around in a studio, but all did not go to plan. "There's literally one of them where he's going 'Get off!'" Kempner told Hawkins. "That's cats for you." Was there friction between the two iconic actors? In an early scene, Sigourney delivers her famous "you little shit-head" line to Boris with real relish. Perhaps she wasn't totally acting in that moment . . .

PYEWACKET

THE SPELL-BINDING FELINE STAR OF CULT CINEMA

Bell, *Book and Candle* is the spell-binding 1958 fantasy rom-com movie starring Kim Novak as Gillian Holroyd (an incredibly chic NYC witch), James Stewart as book publisher and love interest Shep, and Pyewacket, Novak's own gorgeous Siamese playing the part of Gil's familiar.

There is much to delight in this stylish film that imagines the dark glamour of ancient magic amid the beatnik cool of New York's Greenwich Village in the late 1950s. Gil's boutique of African art and Modernist *objet* is deliciously realised, the witch's own apartment interior is just as mouth-watering, and scenes inside the bewitched Zodiac Club reveal it to be the best party venue this side of The Leaky Cauldron. But it is Pyewacket who is at the heart of the story. As Gillian's familiar, he plays a vital role in delivering a love spell to ensnare Shep, padding sinuously past the lens, leaping gracefully from bookcases and stealing every scene.

In 1957 *Bell*'s producers launched a search for the perfect Pyewacket, named after a witch's familiar in British witch trial documents from the 1600s, and film history suggests up to 12 Siamese cats were needed to perform the huge number of magical tricks and stunts. Close-ups of Pyewacket were of a particularly beautiful Siamese cat belonging to legendary animal trainer Frank Inn, who gave him to Novak after the pair formed an otherworldly bond on set.

The plot of *Bell, Book and Candle* are exacting: the glamorous witch, bored with her life, is tantalised with the arrival of her new neighbour, Shep, but must give up the thing she values most – her magical powers – to be able to fall in love. Spoiler alert: Gil must even lose Pyewacket, her true love. At the end, she declares Pye is no longer her cat, and Shep realises Gil's love for him is real (whether Shep was worth such a sacrifice remains a mystery). Odd sexual politics notwithstanding, the film is a 100% cat-powered magical romance and, beside the two lead actors, Pyewacket easily casts his own powerful spell over the viewer.

SIAMESE

COLONEL MEOW

THE MOST HIRSUTE CAT IN THE WORLD

HIMALAYAN-
PERSIAN CROSS

There are many accolades a cat can be awarded: medals for bravery and heroism, gongs for morale-building, mouse-kills, longevity and size – but what of a cat's most catty asset, its fur? Meet Colonel Meow (2011–2014), the hairiest cat who ever lived. The smoke-grey Himalayan-Persian cross enjoyed the longest cat fur ever recorded at 23 centimetres, and (unofficially) the best and most consistent scowl.

Rescued by Seattle Persian and Himalayan Rescue, Colonel Meow found his forever home in 2011 with his loving human, social media wunderkind Anne Avey, who kept him well-loved and, more importantly, perfectly groomed. Persian cats need grooming almost every day, usually with a wide-tooth comb rather than a brush, and bathing every 2–3 months, but not every cat enjoys this process and incredible patience and treats are required. Himalayan and Persian cats are affectionate, but not overwhelmingly so, and are quite happy to play independently or lounge in the sunshine.

Of course, the Colonel was soon an internet celebrity himself, his pale green eyes twinkling for his hundreds of thousands of followers, his scowl set in disapproval. "It didn't faze him at all," said Avey in an interview with local media when the Colonel was awarded an entry in the *Guinness World Records* book in 2014. At the time of the award, Avey and the Colonel had recently moved to the bright lights of Hollywood, but he sadly passed away before his star truly started to shine. He is remembered fondly in the *Guinness World Records*, countless Instagram re-posts, memes and the tufts of cat hair.

GOOSE

THE MARVEL-OUS INTERDIMENSIONAL ALIEN CAT

Goose is the delightfully cute, pale marmalade tabby cat of the modern Marvel universe, a fluffy best-friend to Brie Larson's superhero Captain Marvel. But Goose hides a secret other self: a lethal, interdimensional alien monster with tentacles that burst forth from her feline jaws. First known as Chewie in the original Marvel comic books, the cat belonged to Carol Danvers and travelled the universe with her after her transformation to Captain Marvel. When it is suggested Chewie is not a cat at all but instead a dangerous alien predator known as a Flerken, Captain Marvel scoffs at the idea. But she is soon proved wrong.

Chewie's cinematic version is the seemingly mild-mannered Goose. In *Captain Marvel* (2019), directors Anna Boden and Ryan Fleck were keen to flesh out Goose's character, in the hopes of harnessing the support of the cat-internet, but admit to approaching each Goose scene with trepidation. The film's star, Brie Larson, is allergic to cats, and feline actors are, well, impossible to herd. They found

their star in Reggie. Trainer Ursula Brauner brought him into an audition in his cat bed like some Hollywood starlet. "Reggie hung out on the bed and was as chill as any cat could be, and the filmmakers saw him embody the character then and there," Brauner told the *New York Times*. With an expanded role, three other cats, Archie, Gonzo and Rizzo, were enlisted to support Reggie. "We had enough cat experience to know that cats do not ever do what you want them to do," Boden told *USA Today* on the film's release. The directors had "extraordinarily low expectations" of their cat star, but Reggie seriously impressed. "We found that at times he was more directable than some of the actors we've worked with," said Boden.

There was huge expectation weighing on *Captain Marvel*, and once the film was announced, bro-dude Marvel fans were lukewarm about a female superhero. But Boden and Fleck were right to throw the spotlight on Goose. She has become a beloved member of the franchise, and some consider some of the film's success to be due in part to Reggie's understated performance.

FAITH

THE FUTURE-PREDICTING CHURCH CAT

TABBY

To London, 1941, and a tiny near-magical cat named Faith who lived in the ancient church of St Augustine, a few steps from St Paul's Cathedral. There has been a church on Watling Street since the 1100s – although once destroyed in the Great Fire of 1666, it was rebuilt by famed architect Sir Christopher Wren in 1683. More than 250 years later, a stray tabby cat named Faith liked to wander its pews. She was adopted by the congregation and soon had a single black-and-white kitten, known as Panda.

In 1941, in the midst of the Second World War, London was mired in the Blitz (the systematic bombing of the city). One September day, Faith seemed out of sorts and was seen by Father Henry Ross moving her kitten to the dark, dirty basement of the church. She was soon brought back to the warmth of the church building, but the cat will do what it wants, and the pair kept returning to the basement. In the end, Faith's human friends let her do what she wished and the verger's wife, Rosalind, moved Faith's cat bed down into the dark for comfort.

The following night, during a deathly air raid that killed 400 Londoners, the church was in flames. Four floors had fallen through, and firefighters told a distraught Father Ross that no one, not even a cat, could have survived the blast. But searching through the rubble, Ross called out for Faith and thought he heard a meow. He was delighted to discover Faith and Panda, scuffed but unharmed, still in the same spot in the basement.

Faith's incredible story of survival (not to mention her future-predicting feline wits) became something of an inspirational story to the war-torn city. In 1945 she was awarded an honorary Dickin Medal and citation for bravery (even though she wasn't a military cat) at a ceremony attended by the Archbishop of Canterbury. Father Ross had Faith's photograph taken and put up on the chapel wall with text that read: "Our dear little church cat . . . the bravest cat in the world."

ABOUT DAN JONES

Dan Jones is a bestselling author and dog-lover. He lives in London and writes about booze, grooming, style, queer culture, Princess Diana, and why dogs are so ace.

ACKNOWLEDGEMENTS

Big-pawed thanks to cat consultant Cate Hall, Alex Andreou, Matt Tomlinson, Kate Pollard, Evi O and her studio, and all at Welbeck.

Published in 2023 by OH Editions,
an imprint of Welbeck Non-Fiction Ltd,
part of the Welbeck Publishing Group.

Offices in London,
20 Mortimer Street, London, W1T 3JW,
and Sydney, 205 Commonwealth Street,
Surry Hills, 2010.

www.welbeckpublishing.com

Design © 2023 OH Editions
Text © 2023 Dan Jones
Illustrations © 2023 Evi-O.Studio

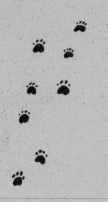

A CIP catalogue record for this book
is available from the British Library.

ISBN 978-1-91431-788-0

Publisher: Kate Pollard
Editor: Matt Tomlinson
Designer: Evi-O.Studio | Kait Polkinghorne & Emi Chiba
Illustrator: Evi-O.Studio | Emi Chiba & Kait Polkinghorne
Production controller: Jess Brisley
Printed and bound by Leo Paper

MIX
Paper | Supporting
responsible forestry
FSC® C020056

10 9 8 7 6 5 4 3 2 1

Disclaimer